THIS BOOK BELONGS TO:

_____

WELCOME TO CONNECTICUT

Dedicated to all the explorers.

All rights reserved.
No part of this book may be reproduced in any form or by any means, electronic or mechanical, and no photocopying or recording, unless you have written permission from the author.

ISBN 978-1-958985-75-5

Text copyright © 2025 by Mimi Jones

www.joeysavestheday.com

A Mimi Book

The name "Connecticut" comes from a Native American word that means "beside the long tidal river." It honors the mighty Connecticut River, which flows through the heart of the state, bringing life, stories, and connection to the land.

-Connecticut River

-Haddam, Connecticut

Connecticut was the fifth state to join the Union. It officially joined on January 9, 1788.

Connecticut is located in the Northeastern region of the United States and is bordered by three states: Massachusetts, Rhode Island, and New York.

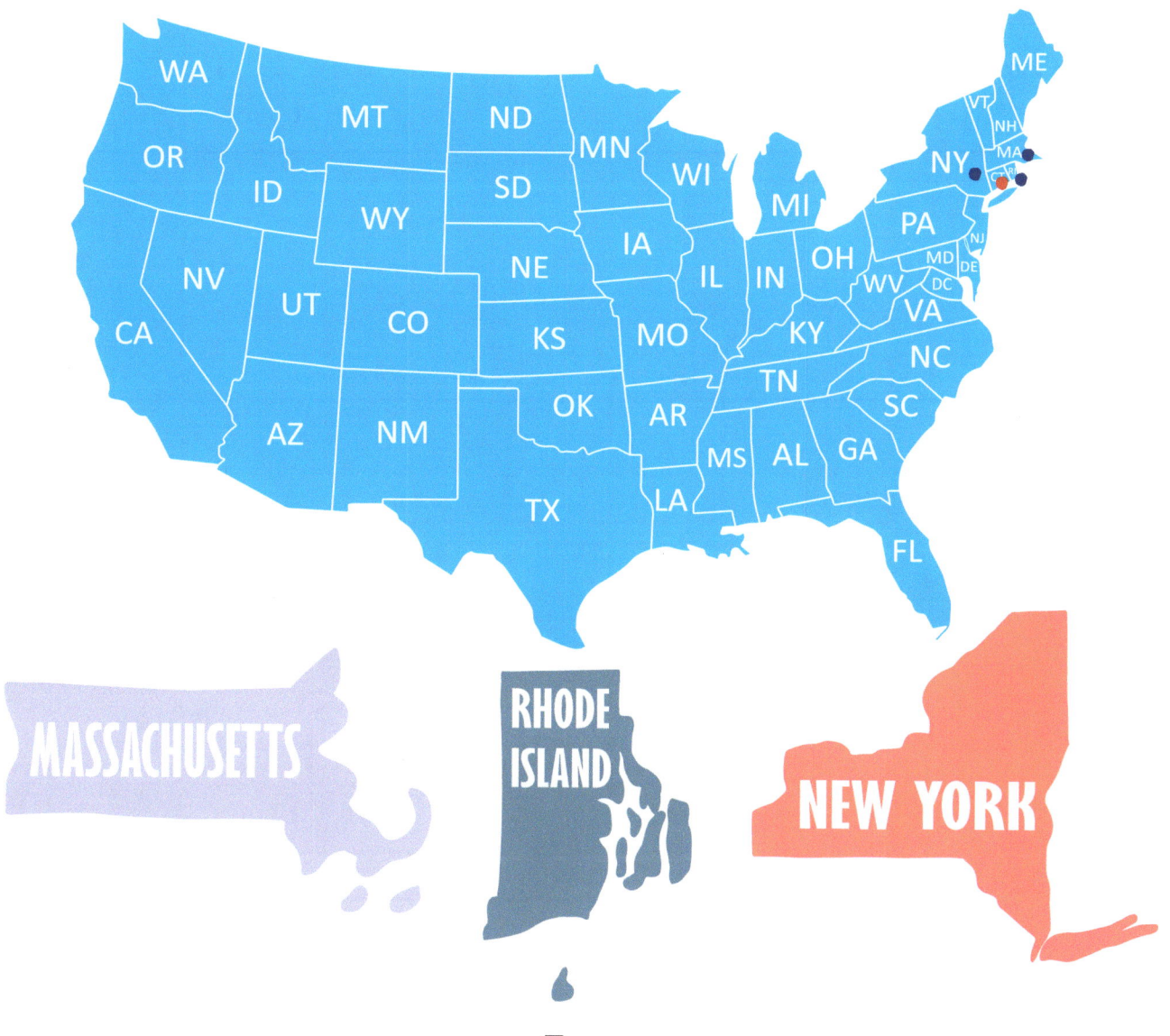

Hartford is the capital of Connecticut.
It officially became the capital in 1875.

Hartford, Connecticut, has an estimated population of about 122,120 people.

Connecticut is the third smallest state in the United States, making it one of the smallest states in the country.

Meriden, Connecticut

There are approximately 3,605,940 people residing in the state of Connecticut.

Milford, Connecticut

Harriet Beecher Stowe was born in Litchfield, Connecticut! She grew up to become a famous author and changemaker. Harriet wrote Uncle Tom's Cabin, a powerful book that helped people understand how wrong slavery was. Her words opened hearts and sparked conversations across the country. Even leaders like President Abraham Lincoln admired her courage. Harriet showed that stories can help people stand up for what's right.

Back in 1878, something amazing happened in New Haven, Connecticut: a tiny book was printed with just 50 names. It was the very first telephone book! People didn't have smartphones or contact lists back then. If you wanted to call someone, you flipped through this little book to find their number. It was the beginning of a whole new way to stay connected, one ring at a time!

Connecticut

There are eight counties in Connecticut.

Here is a list of those counties:

Fairfield
Hartford
Litchfield
Middlesex
New Haven
New London
Tolland
Windham

Mystic Seaport is located in Mystic, Connecticut, along the banks of the Mystic River. It's part of the southeastern shoreline, not far from the Rhode Island border.

Avery Point Light is a small lighthouse in Groton, Connecticut, near the edge of the University of Connecticut's Avery Point campus. Built in 1943, it stands by the water with views of Long Island Sound.

The Bulkeley Bridge stretches across the Connecticut River in Hartford, Connecticut. Built in 1908, it's one of the oldest bridges still used on the Interstate Highway System. Made of strong granite and graceful arches, it was named after Morgan Bulkeley, a former governor and U.S. senator. The bridge connects Hartford and East Hartford.

1908

Weir Farm National Historical Park is tucked into the quiet countryside of Wilton and Ridgefield, Connecticut. It honors J. Alden Weir, a famous American painter who loved painting outdoors. The park is filled with gardens, forests, and art studios, where visitors can walk, explore, and even make their own art. It's the only national park in the U.S. dedicated to American Impressionist painting, blending creativity and nature in a peaceful, inspiring way.

The Connecticut state bird is the American Robin. It was chosen as the state bird in 1943.

The official Connecticut state flower is the Mountain Laurel. It was chosen as the state flower in 1907.

Connecticut's nickname is the Constitution State.

-the-

STATE

Connecticut's official motto, "Qui transtulit sustinet," translates to "He who transplanted is still sustaining."

Avery Point, Groton, Connecticut

Connecticut's state flag was officially adopted on September 9, 1897.

Some crops grown in Connecticut are apples, barley, beets, hay, spinach, and tomatoes.

Some animals that live in Connecticut are black bears, badgers, beavers, coyotes, and deer.

Connecticut experiences significant temperature extremes throughout the year. The highest temperature ever recorded in the state reached an impressive 106 degrees Fahrenheit in Danbury on July 15, 1995. In stark contrast, the record low was -32 degrees Fahrenheit, set in Falls Village on February 16, 1943.

ZOO

Connecticut's Beardsley Zoo is located in Bridgeport, Connecticut, and it's the state's only zoo. Families can explore habitats filled with red pandas, Amur leopards, Mexican gray wolves, bison, and golden lion tamarins.

Gillette Castle State Park is located in East Haddam, Connecticut, overlooking the Connecticut River. The castle was built by actor William Gillette, famous for playing Sherlock Holmes, and looks like a medieval fortress with secret doors and quirky features.

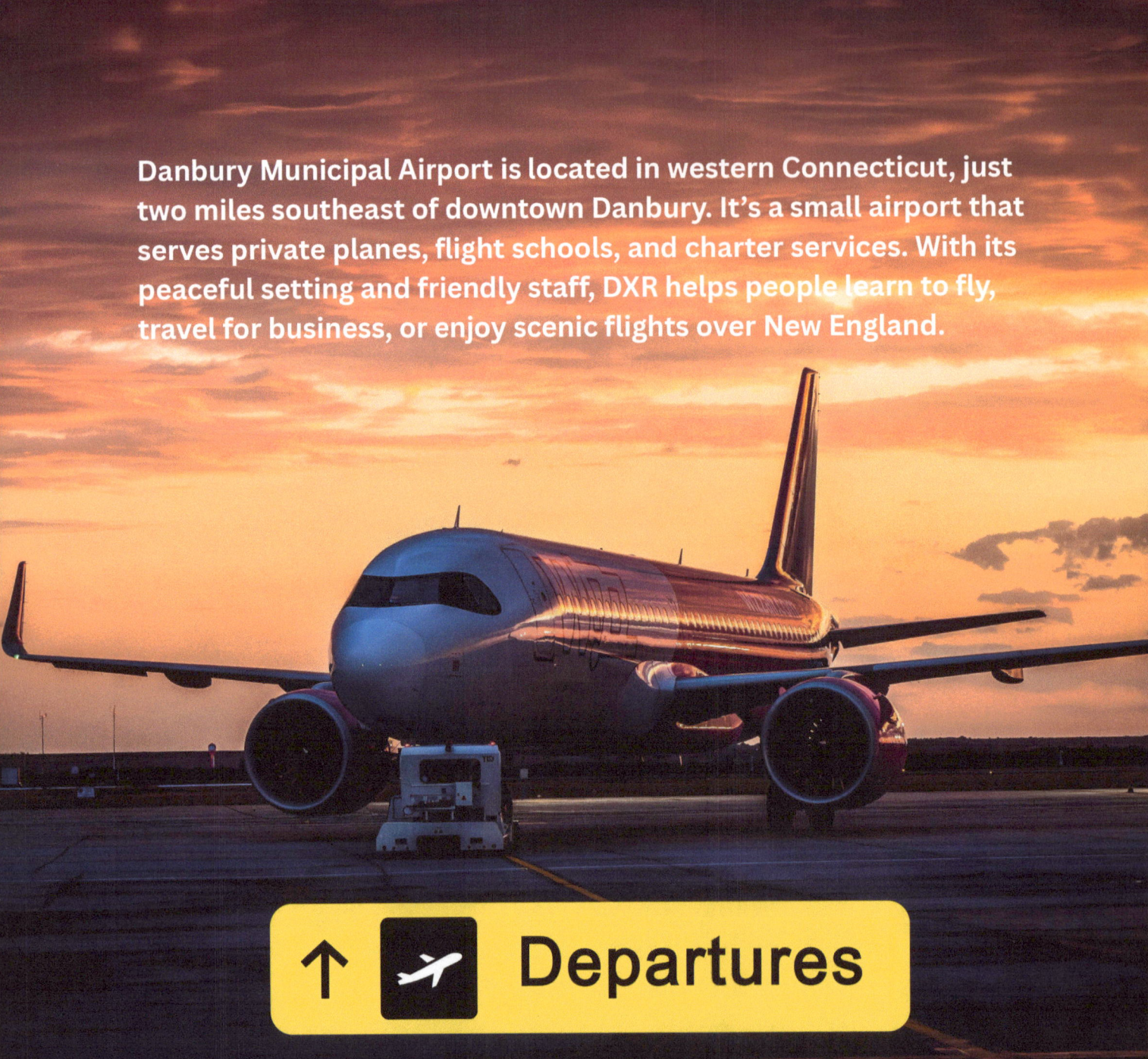

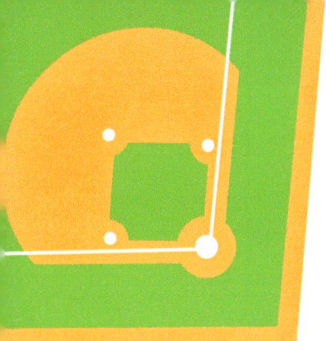

The Norwich Sea Unicorns are a summer baseball team in Norwich, Connecticut. They play at Dodd Stadium and bring fun, teamwork, and sea creature magic to the game.

FOOTBALL

The UConn Huskies are a college football team from Storrs, Connecticut. They represent the University of Connecticut and play home games at Pratt & Whitney Stadium in East Hartford. The team wears blue and white and is known for its determination and school pride.

Connecticut's state tree is the white oak, known for its strength and beauty. One famous white oak, the Charter Oak, helped protect the colony's freedom. In 1687, leaders hid an important paper, the charter, inside the tree to keep it safe from the king's men. That brave act made the Charter Oak a symbol of courage, and today, the white oak reminds us to stand up for what's right.

Connecticut's official state fish is the American Shad. This silvery fish swims from the ocean into rivers like the Connecticut River every spring to lay its eggs. Long ago, it was an important food for Native tribes and early settlers.

Can you name these?

I hope you enjoyed learning about Connecticut.

To explore fun facts about the other 49 states, visit my website at www.joeysavestheday.com. You'll also find a wide variety of homeschool resources to support joyful learning at home. If you enjoyed this book, I would be grateful if you left a review. Your feedback truly helps. Thank you for your support!

Check out these other interesting books in the 50 States Fact Books Series!

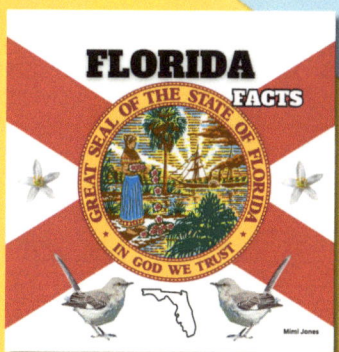

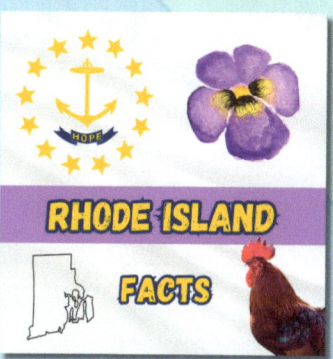

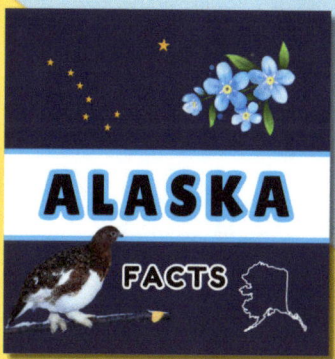

www.mimibooks.com

www.ingramcontent.com/pod-product-compliance
Lightning Source LLC
Chambersburg PA
CBHW040027050426
42453CB00002B/32